The Michigan State University Experience

Written and Compiled by Robert Bao

Artwork by Carolyn Scott Risk

COLLEGE DAYS PRESS

Indianapolis

The Michigan State University Experience

FIRST EDITION

Text © 2001 by Robert Bao
Artwork © 2001 by Carolyn Scott Risk

Produced by R. J. Berg & Company, Publishers, Inc. /College Days Press
under permission from Michigan State University Licensing programs.
All Michigan State University trademarks and images are owned
by Michigan State University.

ISBN 0-89730-211-7

Publisher: R. J. Berg
Series Editor: Ginny Berg

COLLEGE DAYS PRESS
P. O. Box 90235
Indianapolis, IN 46290-0235
Phone 317.251.4640 or 1.888.288.2374
E-mail r.j.berg@worldnet.att.net

Printed in Italy

Front cover illustration: Beaumont Tower
Back cover illustration: Sparty Statue

Contents

Illustrations

Acknowledgments

BEGGAR'S BANQUET – Bob Adler, proprietor

CORAL GABLES – Alex Vanis, proprietor

COWLES HOUSE – First Lady Joanne McPherson; Chef Patrick Merz

DUSTY'S CELLAR– Dusty Rhodes, proprietor; Chef Kevin Cronin

FACULTY FOLK CLUB – Laura Wilkinson, contributor, *Spartan Specialties*

George Perles, former MSU football coach

KRESGE ART MUSEUM – Susan Bandes, director; Dee Cook, contributor, *The Tasteful Palette*

MSU DAIRY STORE – John Engstrom, dairy plant manager

MSU MUSEUM'S CHOCOLATE PARTY – Kurt Dewhurst, director; Joanne McPherson,
contributor, *Chocolate Lover's Companion*

MSU RESIDENCE HALLS – Chuck Gagliano, MSU assistant vice president of housing and food services;
Bruce Haskell, MSU coordinator of food services

MSU UNION HERITAGE CAFÉ – Executive Chef James A. Gray II; Sous Chef Lloyd Thompson

PEANUT BARREL – Joe Bell, proprietor

STATE ROOM, KELLOGG CENTER – Executive Chef Eric Petersen; Executive Sous Chef Rajeev Patgaonkar

TIP-OFF CAFÉ, BRESLIN CENTER – Courtney Craig, manager; Robert Beardsley, proprietor,
and Chef Susan Waterman, Oasis Catering, Grand Haven, Michigan

UNIVERSITY CLUB – Chef John Findley; Sous Chef Shawn Heimitz

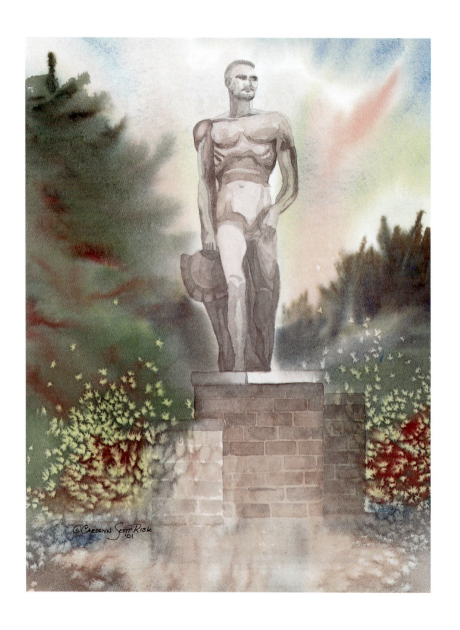

©Carolyn Scott Risk '01

Introduction

Michigan State University is a special place, where learning is enhanced by a truly gorgeous campus, friendly people, state-of-the-art facilities, and a pervasive sense of the school's unique role in history.

Those who spent their formative years on campus—some 350,000 alumni worldwide—can attest to MSU's magical spell. Though they enjoy the highest success in every industry—from autos to film; in classrooms, boardrooms, and labs; from farm fields to fields of dreams—they still yearn to revisit their alma mater. Even first-time visitors, charmed by the Eden-like ambience, often feel these same emotions.

What makes Michigan State so beloved by so many? The best way to find out is simply by visiting. You'll experience love at first sight when you see the panoply of colors within the campus's 5,192 acres, which brim with every imaginable variety of trees and flowers. Countless scenic spots abound—the hollow in Circle Drive, the gazebo in Beal Garden, the

Rose Garden, or the cascading Red Cedar River. Take a canoe ride down the river and you'll see people standing along the lush green banks, feeding the ducks.

Memories are awakened by some six hundred buildings—both historic and modern, classrooms and dorms—where legendary professors passed along knowledge, lifelong friendships were forged, and lots of fun took place, often spontaneously.

Get inspiration from the beautiful artwork that depicts MSU history, such as the Bob Brent murals in Agriculture Hall. Admire the dignity with which Sparty stands as sentinel for MSU's vast athletic complex—Spartan Stadium, Breslin Center, Jenison Fieldhouse, and Munn Arena—and with good reason. MSU is the only Division I school that has won multiple national championships in men's basketball, football, and ice hockey. Listen to the dulcet melodies from the carillons of Beaumont Tower, erected where the nation's first building for teaching scientific agriculture once stood. Coeds who are kissed there at midnight sustain a time-honored tradition.

Watch the bustle in classes and in labs, where scientists discovered myriad breakthroughs, from anticancer drugs to galaxies. Feel the camaraderie in residence halls, the cultural ferment at Wharton Center, and the infectious excitement during activities at the MSU Union. Take part in the goings-on that intellectually and socially engage some forty-three thousand students and four thousand faculty every day. And, yes, take time to enjoy ice cream (or chocolate cheese) at the dairy store.

Visit on a crisp, autumn Saturday afternoon. You'll be aroused by the sounds, pageantry, and aromas of tailgating, as alumni rumble into town flying green and white "S" flags and set up barbecues everywhere. Enjoy the lively music of the MSU Marching Band. Chant "Go Green!" or "Go White!" and join in the outpouring of Spartan spirit during the game.

Read the testimonials of Patriarchs—those who graduated fifty or more years ago—during their annual spring reunion. "The campus I found incredibly beautiful," writes Richard O'Brien, class of 1936, recounting the day he arrived on campus from Port Austin. "Felt that I was on an estate of the wealthiest man in the United States."

Finally, stop and ask for directions. Everyone has to, from time to time. Chances are you'll receive help with a courteous smile. People matter at the university that pioneered the democratization of higher education in America.

Today, the nation's pioneer land-grant college is a megaversity with two cyclotrons, three medical colleges, a new law school, and a powerful telescope in the Chilean Andes. But MSU's emphasis on people, ultimately, explains why the Michigan State experience continues to tug our hearts.

MSU's Rich History

Few universities have a heritage as significant as that at MSU, the nation's first "accessible" college. The dramatic postwar growth that transformed it into a global research university remains unmatched to this day.

The "school that's known to all" began humbly in 1855, when Michigan governor Kingsley Bingham approved the creation of an agricultural college in East Lansing. Two years later, classes began with five faculty members and sixty-three students—the nation's first step in making higher learning accessible to farmers and workers.

In 1862, access broadened when President Abraham Lincoln signed the Morrill Act, authorizing the creation of land-grant universities throughout the country. MSU emerged as the nation's model land-grant school, teaching agricultural science and mechanics, conducting research, and transmitting useful knowledge to the state's citizens.

President Theodore Roosevelt touted MSU's national role during his commencement address at the school in 1907—yet he probably could not have foreseen MSU's epic rise following World War II.

It was during the presidency of John A. Hannah (1941–69) that MSU took its present form. He led a construction boom that expanded MSU to fourteen degree-granting colleges with twenty-seven dorms containing eight thousand–plus rooms, and enrollment leaped from six thousand to more than forty thousand. Piece by piece, Hannah assembled the mosaic that would complete his master plan. He amassed land, attracted top scholars and students, and spearheaded MSU's entry into the Big Ten athletic conference in 1949 after elevating athletics, notably football, to national prominence. He extended MSU's reach with global projects. After President Hannah retired, it was said that cement mixers churned for a month in his honor.

Today, MSU is a research-intensive university where scientists have made many discoveries, such as homogenized milk, hybrid corn, cisplatin (world's leading anticancer drug), indoor turfgrass, and the universe's largest galaxy. In 1993, MSU president Peter McPherson launched a new wave of productivity. He extended access through a Tuition Guarantee, maneuvered to enhance state support, and brought a law school to campus. Many new buildings loom, including a massive science complex. Entering the new millennium, the cement mixers continue to churn—but with a master plan in place, Spartans can rest assured that the treasured MSU campus will remain as beautiful as ever.

Campus Landmarks

No MSU landmark evokes more recognition than Beaumont Tower, a splendorous Collegiate Gothic structure marking the original site of College Hall, America's first building for teaching scientific agriculture. The forty-seven-bell carillon contained within the 1929 tower continues its daily chiming. In 1945, sculptor Leonard Jungwirth unveiled the Sparty ceramic statue as a welcome beacon to postwar students. The Rock, a gift from the class of 1873, located just north of the river and east of the Farm Lane bridge, has evolved from geological specimen to a forum reflecting the vicissitudes of student opinion. Near Linton Hall, a two-sided fountain-trough recalls bygone horse-and-buggy days. MSU's oldest building is the 1857 Alice Cowles House, built in Victorian style with bricks made of clay from the banks of the Red Cedar River. Joseph Williams, MSU's first president, lived there. In 1941, the historic landmark became MSU's official presidential residence.

Spartan Spirit French Toast

*S*ince 1993, MSU president Peter McPherson and his wife Joanne have opened wide the doors of Cowles House, averaging some 140 university events a year for faculty, students, alumni, and friends. Among the most popular items served is Spartan Spirit French Toast.

---

1 cup packed brown sugar

½ cup (1 stick) unsalted butter

2 tablespoons pure maple syrup

6 to 8 thick slices white bread, crusts removed

1½ cups half-and-half

5 large eggs

2 teaspoons Kahlúa coffee liqueur

1 teaspoon vanilla

¼ teaspoon salt

In a small, heavy saucepan, combine brown sugar, butter, and maple syrup; cook over medium heat, stirring constantly, until butter melts and mixture is smooth and well blended. Pour into a 13x9x2-inch baking dish. Arrange slices of bread in one layer over brown sugar–butter mixture (do not overlap bread slices). In a mixing bowl, combine half-and-half, eggs, Kahlúa, vanilla, and salt; whisk until well blended. Pour mixture evenly over bread in baking dish. Cover and refrigerate for at least 8 hours or overnight.

Preheat oven to 350°F. Remove cover from baking dish and bake in the middle of the oven for about 35 to 45 minutes or until the edges are golden brown. Cut into squares and serve immediately.

Yield: 6 to 8 servings

The Saga of Johnny Marzetti

MSU students have always loved pranks. Historian Madison Kuhn wrote of "barrels filled with iron wedges rolled mysteriously down dormitory stairs late at night . . ." Bells used for signaling mealtimes were turned upside down and filled with water so the puller would be drenched. And students often raided neighboring farms, filling their overalls with contraband apples, cherries, or a watermelon. In the '50s and '60s, dorm residents loved a beef casserole dish called Johnny Marzetti. But when pranksters began to spread ghoulish rumors about the ingredients in the casserole, students stopped eating it—so it was removed from the menu. A few years later, however, the dish was quietly reintroduced as Italian Noodle Bake, and the students loved it! And so, MSU's culinary Lazarus is once again unabashedly called Johnny Marzetti.

Johnny Marzetti

*D*ating from the 1920s, this casserole is the ultimate comfort food. Many baby boomers will have memories of this dish, which was popular with their working moms. The rumormongers could not have picked on a more innocent target, but thankfully, university officials restored it to its proper place— on the menu.

1½ quarts water	2 teaspoons beef bouillon granules
1 teaspoon vegetable oil	1 teaspoon dried oregano leaves
5 ounces extra wide noodles	½ teaspoon dried basil leaves
1½ pounds ground beef	½ teaspoon minced fresh garlic
1 cup diced sweet green pepper (2 medium peppers)	½ teaspoon garlic powder
½ cup chopped celery (1 rib celery)	½ teaspoon garlic salt
½ cup chopped onion (1 small onion)	½ teaspoon salt
1 quart water	½ teaspoon pepper
1 can (6 ounces) tomato paste	1 cup shredded sharp cheddar cheese

Bring 1½ quarts water to a rolling boil in a large pot; add oil and noodles. Cook noodles al dente, about 3 to 4 minutes. Drain noodles and rinse with cold water. Drain again, then set aside.

Brown ground beef in a large skillet; drain excess fat. Add all remaining ingredients except cheese; mix well. Simmer uncovered on low heat for 20 minutes, stirring occasionally.

Preheat oven to 350°F. Grease a two-quart casserole. Add cooked noodles to ground beef mixture; stir to mix. Adjust seasonings, if necessary. Transfer mixture to prepared casserole; sprinkle cheese over top. Bake uncovered at 350°F for 20 minutes. Remove from oven and let sit for 5 to 10 minutes before serving.

Yield: 8 to 10 servings

MSU Gardens

---

*E*xplosions of colors and heady scents recur every spring as more than nine thousand species and varieties of flowers and plants come to life on campus. The MSU Gardens have provided inspiration for countless Spartans, as well as composer Ellen Taaffe Zwilich, whose Symphony No. 4 "The Gardens" recaptures the gardens' lushness. The oldest—and recently named "most romantic"—is the W. J. Beal Botanical Garden (1873), which features plant labels, buried seed bottles, and a gazebo. In the Horticultural Demonstration Gardens (1993), a statue of Liberty Hyde Bailey, the Father of American Horticulture, stands amid annuals, perennials, roses, and other plants. The 4-H Children's Garden, one of five demonstration gardens, has been called "the most creative half-acre in America." The Clarence E. Lewis Landscape Arboretum features many themes, including a Japanese garden. A detour through any garden on the way to class offers a marvelous respite from exams.

Mint Chocolate Chip Ice Cream

*D*uring relaxing strolls across campus, many students swing by the MSU Dairy Store in Anthony Hall for a scoop of ice cream. Some special additions to your favorite ice cream mix are what make Mint Chocolate Chip a favorite . . . and give it just the right Spartan color.

Ice Cream

Homemade ice cream mix
   (use your favorite recipe or see below)

Peppermint extract (start with a few drops,
   adjusting amount to taste)

Green food coloring (start with several drops,
   adding more if a darker green is desired)

½ cup (4 ounces) chocolate chips

American Egg Board's Frozen Custard Ice Cream Mix

For 1½ to 2 quarts mix:

6 eggs

2 cups milk

¾ cup sugar

2 to 3 tablespoons honey

¼ teaspoon salt

2 cups whipping cream

1 tablespoon vanilla

To prepare Frozen Custard Ice Cream Mix: In a medium saucepan, beat together eggs, milk, sugar, honey, and salt. Cook over low heat, stirring constantly, until mixture is thick enough to coat a metal spoon with a thin film and temperature reaches at least 160°F. Cool quickly by setting pan in ice or cold water and stirring for a few minutes. Cover and refrigerate until custard is thoroughly chilled, at least 1 hour.

To prepare Ice Cream: When ready to freeze, combine chilled custard, whipping cream, and vanilla. Add peppermint extract until desired flavor is reached. Add green food coloring until desired color is reached. Pour mixture into an ice cream maker (electric or hand-operated) and freeze according to manufacturer's instructions. Stir chocolate chips into soft ice cream.

Yield: 8 to 10 servings

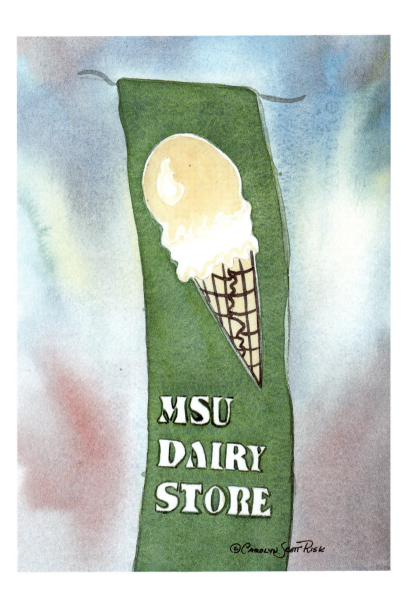

MSU
DAIRY
STORE

©CAROLYN SCOTT RISK

Kellogg Center

Looming tall across from the Brody complex, the Kellogg Hotel and Conference Center opened in 1952 to serve many purposes. It provides students of *The* School of Hospitality Business with hands-on labs and training. It serves continuing education needs. It's the home of the MSU Alumni Association's Evening College, which offers noncredit courses ranging from Haiku Poetry to the History of Broadway Musicals. After major renovations, this state-of-the-art center boasts 165 rooms—many with gorgeous views of the Red Cedar—an auditorium, lecture halls, thirty-five thousand square feet of flexible space, and even satellite hookups. Food service here remains unmatched. The State Room, with an aromatic coffee bar, ranks among East Lansing's top restaurants. Casual visitors might prefer sampling a corned beef sandwich at the deli and pasta bar of the River Café, or enjoying a postgame libation in the cozy Spartan Pub to celebrate the latest MSU victory.

Michigan Bean Soup

*V*isitors and returning alums love to dine in the beautiful and elegant State Room at Kellogg Center. After several decades on the menu, the delicious Michigan Bean Soup remains its signature item.

1 pound dried navy beans

2 tablespoons butter

½ cup diced carrot (1 medium carrot)

½ cup diced celery (1 rib celery)

½ cup diced onion (1 small onion)

10 cups water

1 cup diced smoked ham

3 bay leaves

2 tablespoons ham-flavored soup base

1 teaspoon dried thyme leaves

2 fresh ripe tomatoes, diced

1 can (14 ounces) diced tomatoes

1 cup cubed potato (1 medium potato)

Salt and pepper

*Garnishes: Chopped fresh parsley and
    diced fresh tomatoes*

Place navy beans in a large bowl or saucepan and add enough water to cover. Set aside to soak for 8 to 10 hours or overnight.

Melt butter in a soup pot set over medium heat. Add carrot, celery, and onion; sauté for about 3 to 5 minutes or until onion is transparent. Drain beans and add to soup pot along with water, ham, bay leaves, soup base, and thyme. Bring to a boil over high heat, then reduce heat to low. Cover and cook for 1½ hours, stirring occasionally. Add fresh tomatoes, canned tomatoes, and potato; cook 15 to 20 minutes longer, stirring occasionally. Season with salt and pepper. Garnish each serving with a sprinkle of chopped parsley and 1 tablespoon diced tomatoes.

Yield: 20 servings

©CAROLYN Scott RISK
'01

Life on Campus

New students might be awed by MSU's size at first, but they soon engage fully in campus life. They grow, thrive, find their way around ninety-nine miles of paths, pursue their passions, and learn to live—and, perhaps, love.

An incredible vitality rises from the annual arrival of thousands of new and returning students, who hail from every county in Michigan, every state in the Union, and more than one hundred foreign countries. Years later, many will remember these felicitous times as "the best years of my life."

Newcomers proceed to decorate the dorm room, figure out the system and the lay of the land, choose courses, meet new friends, and get used to bunk beds and sharing bathrooms. They actually meet professors, whether in a freshman seminar or as a research assistant. New ideas bombard them like the riot of autumn colors erupting around them.

By the time snow blankets the campus, however, they've settled down and discovered MSU's vast resources. Future lawyers, for example, savor the profession at the state-of-the-art Moot Court in the MSU–Detroit College of Law. Physics majors examine atomic collisions with the world's most powerful accelerator. Agriculture students enjoy "living classrooms," including a huge farm near Gull Lake and the Hidden Lakes Gardens near Jackson. Veterinary medicine students, who starred in the Animal Planet TV network's *Vet School Confidential* series, study horses in a magnificent equine center near Adrian.

When they need a break from studying, students play racquet sports or basketball, swim, or work out in one of many facilities—or they try to birdie the water hole at Forest Akers West, the championship course redesigned by Arthur Hills.

Students learn the "MSU Fight Song" right away, during orientation, along with other tips about "What It Means To Be A Spartan." They meet top athletes and the Spartan Marching Band at Spartan Spirit, an annual tradition in Spartan Stadium. Fans maneuver into spirit groups—Bobby's World (football), the Izzone (men's basketball), Slapshots (ice hockey), or Pack Attack (women's basketball).

Some lucky students fall in love. For them, the MSU Alumni Memorial Chapel, built in 1952 to honor more than five hundred Spartans who died while in the armed services, can help seal yet another lifetime bond.

Hitting the Books

*F*or serious studying, students seek secluded recesses and cubicles wherever they can be found. On nice days, some favor outdoor retreats—by the Red Cedar, under a tree in Circle Drive, in the fountain courtyard behind Natural Sciences, or on a manicured lawn behind the International Center. There are benches at the Horticultural Demonstration Gardens, if one is not distracted by all of the glorious colors. When the weather sends you indoors, the arched alcoves in the MSU Auditorium offer a view of Charles Pollock murals depicting MSU's land-grant history. Fourteen branch libraries offer cozy spaces, but the Main Library on West Circle Drive also has distractions—such as its special comic books collection and the Vincent Voice Library of taped speeches, interviews, broadcasts, and more. At the MSU Union, comfy nooks lie throughout the lobby; hungry students can venture downstairs to the Heritage Café, where murals of iconic profs offer inspiration for cracking the books.

London Broil

*S*ome folks go to the MSU Union's Heritage Café just to savor the London Broil, the most popular item. Sous Chef Lloyd Thompson says the secret is in the special marinade.

---

1 cup bottled barbecue sauce, divided
1 cup Italian salad dressing, divided
3 pounds flank steak
Hot cooked rice

Combine ½ cup barbecue sauce and ½ cup Italian salad dressing in a resealable plastic bag; squeeze bag gently to blend ingredients. Add steak and squeeze bag gently so steak is completely coated with marinade. Seal bag and place in refrigerator for 8 to 10 hours or overnight.

Preheat grill to high. Remove steak from plastic bag and discard marinade. Grill steak for 8 to 12 minutes on each side or until internal temperature reaches 140°F. Meanwhile, combine remaining barbecue sauce and Italian salad dressing in a small saucepan; heat until mixture is bubbling.

To serve, cut steak across the grain into 1/8-inch slices. Top sliced steak with warm sauce and serve over rice.

Yield: 4 to 6 servings

Hoops, Hopes, and Hoopla

---

*I*n the 1978–79 season, pure frenzy filled Jenison Fieldhouse, longtime home for MSU hoops (until 1990). The season ended with Magic Johnson leading MSU to the 1979 NCAA title. Enthusiasm for MSU hoops has been rekindled under head coach Tom Izzo—and the Flintstones (Charlie Bell, Mateen Cleaves, Morris Peterson, and Antonio Smith, all from Flint), who lit a blaze with four straight Big Ten titles, three straight NCAA Final Fours, and the 2000 NCAA title. Foes dread games played at the Breslin Student Events Center, where they are barraged by taunts from 953 raving students in the Izzone. Equally hostile is Munn Arena, where coach Ron Mason's ice hockey program delivers wins, sellouts, championships, and Hobey Baker awards like daily newspapers. Every fall, fifteen thousand students gather at Spartan Stadium to soak up Spartan Spirit and learn the fight song in preparation for Saturday afternoon action on the gridiron. Rah! Team! Fight! Victory for MSU!

©CAROLYN SCOTT RISK '01

Creole Stew

*B*efore each home basketball game, the Tip-Off Café in Breslin Center's mezzanine serves up a preview from Tom Izzo along with gourmet fare by Oasis Catering of Grand Haven, Michigan. One signature dish is the spicy Creole Stew—a perfect prelude to "hoops on fire"!

½ cup olive oil

2 ribs celery, finely chopped

2 Vidalia onions, finely chopped

2 sweet green peppers, julienned

2 sweet red peppers, julienned

2 bay leaves

1 tablespoon Creole seasoning (or to taste)

1 teaspoon dried thyme leaves

1 pound precooked andouille sausage,
    cut into 2-inch pieces

1 pound boneless, skinless chicken breasts, grilled
    and cut into strips

1 pound cooked shrimp (30–40 count), tail on

4 large, very ripe tomatoes, cut into wedges

3 or 4 splashes hot pepper sauce or Tabasco (or to taste)

Salt and pepper

2 ears sweet corn, cut into 1-inch pieces (optional)

1 small package frozen cut okra

Water or V-8 juice, if needed

Hot cooked rice or orzo

Heat oil in a Dutch oven or large skillet set over medium-high heat. Add celery, onions, green and red peppers, bay leaves, Creole seasoning, and thyme; sauté, stirring often, for about 3 to 5 minutes or until onions are transparent. Add sausage and chicken; cook, stirring often, for about 3 to 5 minutes or until sausage is lightly browned. Add shrimp, tomatoes, hot pepper sauce or Tabasco, salt, pepper, and corn, if desired; continue cooking, stirring constantly, for 2 to 3 minutes.

Add okra and a splash of water or V-8 juice if the mixture looks too dry. Reduce heat, cover pan, and simmer for 3 to 4 minutes. Serve over rice ("dirty" rice is best) or orzo, with a selection of hot sauces on the side.

Yield: 8 servings

Culture and Arts

---

*F*abulous museums, libraries, music halls, and access to some of the nation's top minds—MSU offers abundant exposure to culture and the arts, even when students simply hang out. As MSU undergrads, for example, writers Jim Cash *(Top Gun),* Richard Ford *(Independence Day),* Dan Gerber *(A Last Bridge Home),* Jim Harrison *(Legends of the Fall),* and Tom McGuane *(The Sporting Club)* were regulars at the MSU Union, sipping coffee at the grill's roundtables. Across West Circle Drive, the MSU Museum boasts three floors of spectacular collections, including Great Lakes artifacts, special exhibits on natural and cultural history (plus the on-line Quilt Index), and dramatic dinosaur skeletons. A huge, upright brown bear in the lobby never fails to awe visiting youngsters. Just off Farm Lane, the Kresge Art Museum houses more than sixty-five hundred works of art, including Dali's *Remorse,* Rodin's *Figure Volante,* and Calder's *Sunrise Over The Pyramid.*

Chocolate Sour Cream Fudge Cake

*E*very February, the MSU Museum's Chocolate Party yields mouth-watering recipes, gathered in the Chocolate Lover's Companion. *At the twelfth annual benefit in 2001, MSU First Lady Joanne McPherson contributed one of her favorites—this rich fudge cake recipe.*

---

2 cups flour	4 ounces unsweetened chocolate, melted and cooled
2 teaspoons baking soda	1½ teaspoons pure vanilla
½ teaspoon salt	1 cup dairy sour cream
2¼ cups packed light or dark brown sugar	1 cup very strong hot brewed coffee
½ cup (1 stick) unsalted butter, softened	Icing (use your favorite recipe)
3 eggs	

Preheat oven to 350°F. Grease two 9-inch square pans and line them with waxed paper; set aside. Sift together flour, baking soda, and salt; set aside. In a mixing bowl, combine brown sugar, butter, and eggs; beat with an electric mixer for 5 minutes or until mixture is very light and fluffy. Beat in chocolate and vanilla. Gradually add dry ingredients alternately with sour cream, beginning and ending with dry ingredients and stirring just until blended after each addition. Add coffee and stir to mix. Pour batter into prepared pans.

To release air bubbles in batter, hold a pan four or five inches above counter top and then drop the pan straight onto the counter, being careful not to tip or spill the batter. Repeat with second pan. Bake at 350°F for 35 minutes. Remove from oven and place pans on a wire rack to cool for 15 minutes. Run a knife around the inside edges of each pan, then turn out cakes; remove waxed paper and cool cakes completely. Frost with your favorite icing.

Yield: 12 to 16 servings

Live and Learn

Students living on campus can really focus on learning. MSU's residence hall system—the nation's largest, some say the finest—takes care of just about every worry. Dorm residents have study areas, cybercafés, convenience stores (open till midnight), plus laundry, exercise, and recreation rooms, even job opportunities. Many dorms include classrooms—great for bad weather days. Phones, cable TV, voice mail, and Internet connections come with no monthly bills. Students use unlimited creativity in decorating their rooms. Bridge, once popular, has been replaced by electronic games such as Crazy Taxi. Some halls—Akers, Brody, Hubbard, Wilson, and Wonders—can each house more than a thousand residents. Weekdays from 7 A.M. to 7 P.M., an incredible array of food is available—fresh fruit, salads, bread from the MSU Bakery, and other award-winning creations. Best of all . . . there are no dishes to wash!

General Tso's Chicken

*S*ome things never change, like macaroni and cheese and Rice Krispies treats, which remain perennial student favorites. In recent years, though, General Tso's Chicken has emerged as the most popular entrée in dorm cafeterias . . . perhaps because it tastes Tso good!

1½ cups chicken broth

½ cup light soy sauce

¼ cup burgundy

¼ cup white wine

¼ cup granulated sugar

⅛ cup packed brown sugar

1 tablespoon minced fresh garlic

1 tablespoon grated fresh ginger

1 teaspoon dark soy sauce

1½ teaspoons crushed red pepper

⅓ cup water

1½ tablespoons cornstarch

1¼ pounds frozen popcorn chicken

1 bunch (8 to 10) green onions, sliced

Hot cooked jasmine rice

In a saucepan, combine chicken broth, light soy sauce, burgundy, white wine, granulated sugar, brown sugar, garlic, ginger, and dark soy sauce; bring to a low boil over medium-high heat. Add red pepper; reduce heat and simmer for 5 minutes. Combine water and cornstarch in a small bowl; whisk to blend. Add cornstarch to sauce and continue cooking, stirring constantly, until mixture thickens. Remove from heat and keep warm.

Fry or bake chicken according to package directions. Add cooked chicken to warm sauce. Garnish with green onions and serve over jasmine rice.

Yield: 6 servings

WHARTON CENTER FOR PE

©CAROLYN Scott Risk
'01

Weekend Escapes

Imagine the luxury of walking across campus to see *Phantom of the Opera*, cellist Yo-Yo Ma, comedian George Carlin, or a Moscow Festival Ballet performance of "Swan Lake." These and a host of other stellar performances enchant audiences at the Wharton Center for Performing Arts, an architectural marvel that heads MSU's cultural landscape—just as *Orpheus*, Mel Leiserowitz's dramatic six-ton steel sculpture, commands its charming entrance plaza.

Weekends offer a zillion options. Whether one wants to party, be entertained, catch up on midterms, hang out with friends, shop, or simply ruminate about life—all escapes are there. Operas, recitals, and plays by the music and theater departments; lectures and symposia staged by academic units; and fabulous museum exhibits all add to MSU's cultural panorama. Dances, movies, and theme events offer social escapes. Breslin Center features everything from rock concerts to Monster trucks. Exotic scents and flavors prevail at global festivals; exotic cars star at the MSU Alumni Association's annual Cars on Campus show. Beyond toga parties, Greeks sponsor many community service projects.

MSU students hear from prominent visiting speakers, such as poet Maya Angelou; historian David McCullough; playwright Arthur Miller; pundit George Will (who once taught at MSU's James Madison College); actress Ann-Margret; novelist and alum Tom McGuane; screenwriter and alum Jack Epps, Jr.; and civil rights leaders Jesse Jackson, Coretta Scott King, and Kweisi Mfume. In September 2000, basketball analyst Dick Vitale infused some "Spartan Spirit" into twenty thousand students at Spartan Stadium.

Sports enthusiasts can participate in intramurals or one of twenty-two varsity teams, or spectate in world-class venues: Breslin Center, Munn Arena, and Spartan Stadium (where a world attendance record was to be set October 6, 2001 for . . . ice hockey!). Many join spirit groups sponsored by the Student Alumni Foundation. And there's more. Bowlers throw strikes in the MSU Union, ice skaters slide and glide at Munn, and horse lovers enjoy equestrian shows at the Pavilion.

Weekends also offer opportunities to explore the campus periphery, from parties and live music entertainment to shopping excursions to the Meridian Mall. During contemplative moments, some seek a private place, perhaps where they can commune with Mother Nature. One can bike, hike, jog, canoe, or simply spread a soft blanket on the riverbank, lie back, and listen to the cascading waters.

The Wharton Center

*L*es *Mis.* Itzhak Perlman. The Vienna Philharmonic. *Riverdance.* The world's best-known performers make pilgrimages to the Wharton Center for Performing Arts, mid-Michigan's premier cultural hub. It opened in 1982, sporting a bold, majestic architectural design. Four ceremonial banners hang in the Grand Foyer, around which are huge angled spaces and elegant lobbies and lounges. The twenty-five-hundred-seat Catherine Herrick Cobb Great Hall boasts fourteen giant acoustic pillars and a fifty-eight-foot proscenium—with enough room for Hannibal and his elephants!—while the Pasant Theatre features a Shakespearean thrust stage. Wharton Center, the resident showcase for MSU's music and theater departments and the Greater Lansing Symphony, attracts students, faculty, and arts lovers from all over the Midwest. In 1992, it gained national attention when the last presidential debate with George Bush, Bill Clinton, and Ross Perot was held in the Great Hall.

Cherry and Pecan Crusted Whitefish

*D*inner at the University Club is a popular preshow option for Wharton Center patrons. Chef John Findley oversees the kitchen, where one of the most popular creations is Sous Chef Shawn Heimitz's Cherry and Pecan Crusted Whitefish.

¾ cup flour

4 eggs

6 tablespoons buttermilk

½ cup dry bread crumbs

4 tablespoons (2 ounces) dried cherries, coarsely chopped

4 tablespoons (2 ounces) pecans, coarsely chopped

4 whitefish fillets, boned (6 ounces each)

2 tablespoons clarified butter

Garnishes: Sherry-Sage Beurre Blanc and cherry syrup (homemade or purchased)

Preheat oven to 400°F. Lightly grease a baking sheet; set aside.

Place flour in a medium-size shallow pan. Break eggs into a second shallow pan and beat lightly. Add buttermilk to eggs and mix well. In a third shallow pan, combine bread crumbs, cherries, and pecans; mix well. Dredge fish in flour, shaking off excess flour. Dip fish in egg mixture, coating completely. Place fish in bread crumb mixture, turning once so both sides are coated. Press the crumb mixture onto the fish so it will not come off during cooking.

Heat butter in a large sauté pan set over medium-high heat. Place the fish, flesh side down, in the skillet and cook for 1 or 2 minutes or until crumb coating starts to brown. Turn over and cook for 1 or 2 minutes. Place fish on prepared baking sheet and bake at 400°F for 8 to 12 minutes. Serve with sherry-sage beurre blanc and cherry syrup.

Yield: 4 servings

Sherry-Sage Beurre Blanc

½ cup sherry

¼ cup white vinegar

½ cup heavy cream

4 tablespoons butter, softened

½ teaspoon dried sage

Salt and pepper

Combine sherry and vinegar in a small, heavy-gauge saucepan. Bring to a slow boil over medium heat and cook for 7 to 10 minutes or until mixture is reduced to about ⅛ to ¼ cup. Add cream and continue cooking over medium heat for 8 to 12 minutes or until sauce thickens. Reduce heat to low and add butter, mixing with a whisk until butter is completely melted. Add sage, salt, and pepper; stir to blend. Remove from heat and keep warm.

Yield: 1 cup

©Carolyn Scott Risk '01

A-Lot of Tailgating

"Kill, Bubba, Kill!" was the chant in the halcyon 1960s, when Spartan teams fought with a vim. On football Saturdays, autumn hues of orange and rust bathe the campus, and student and alumni tailgaters converge on Spartan Stadium, ever optimistic about victory. With green "S" flags flying on cars and campers, they bring tents, folding chairs, and provisions. The aroma of grilled ribs fills the air. The Spartan Marching Band rouses emotions during rehearsal at Walter Adams Field. As the football players stride from Kellogg Center to the North Tunnel, loud cheers erupt along the procession, from the A-Lot to the jazz stand of the Geriatric Six. Many enthusiasts stop by the alumni tent to collect prizes, play games, get their faces painted, and perhaps spot former stars such as Tico Duckett, Kirk Gibson, and Lorenzo White. Soak up the atmosphere, for Spartan teams are bound to win!

Kugelis

*B*ored with potato salad? Try kugelis, as prepared by former MSU football coach George Perles. This classic Lithuanian dish will nourish tailgaters on even the most unseasonably cool, frosty days.

5 pounds Idaho potatoes
2 large onions
6 eggs, beaten
1 cup (2 sticks) butter, melted
½ pound bacon
Dairy sour cream

Preheat oven to 350°F. Grease a 9x13-inch baking pan; set aside.

Peel and grate potatoes and onions. (Do not use a blender for grating—use the fine side of a hand grater.) Combine grated potatoes and onions in a mixing bowl; add eggs and butter and mix well. Spread mixture in prepared pan. Bake at 350°F for 1½ to 2 hours or until golden brown.

While kugelis is baking, fry bacon until crisp; drain and crumble. Cut warm kugelis into squares to serve. Top each serving with a dollop of sour cream and a sprinkle of bacon.

Yield: 10 to 12 servings

Note: You can bake this a day ahead and then refrigerate it. Reheat before serving. If you'll be serving it at a tailgate party, place aluminum foil on a grill and spray lightly with nonstick cooking spray. Place the kugelis on the foil to heat, turning once.

The Campus Center

*F*irst-run movies—such as *Traffic, American Pie,* and *Sixth Sense*—for free! *With* popcorn and munchies (at reasonable prices). Dances with live music, video parties, mixers, crafts such as glass etching and pottery painting, and jousting (with gigantic Q-tips). Not enough? How about inflatable sumo wrestling? Or pretending to be the next Carrot Top, or Chris Rock, or Rita Rudner at a comedy show? MSU students have all these options at a weekend entertainment complex anchored at the International Center and Wells Hall. Though its name is nondescript, the center attracts more than two thousand students each weekend, about sixty thousand per year. Under the aegis of the University Activities Board, it provides loads of fun in an alcohol-free setting. Plenty of refreshments and food are available at the Crossroads Food Court, which stays open till 1 a.m.—just in case all that sumo wrestling whetted the appetite.

Summer Pasta

*T*his recipe from Dee Cook, MSU trustee and benefactor, appeared in Kresge Art Museum's cookbook, The Tasteful Palette. *"I just looked in the refrigerator to see what was there and this recipe was the result,"* she explains. *"It's still a family favorite."*

---

8 Roma tomatoes, chopped

1 ripe avocado, peeled and diced

⅓ cup chopped fresh basil

2 tablespoons chopped fresh cilantro (or to taste)

1 or 2 cloves garlic, chopped

¼ cup olive oil (or to taste)

½ cup crumbled feta cheese

Salt and pepper

8 ounces linguine (or your favorite pasta)

Garnish: Grated Parmesan or Asiago cheese (optional)

Combine tomatoes and avocado in a mixing bowl. Add basil, cilantro, and garlic; mix gently. Drizzle oil over tomato mixture and toss lightly so all ingredients are well moistened. Add feta cheese, salt, and pepper; stir gently with a rubber spatula. Cover and let sit for about 1 hour so the flavors will marry.

Cook pasta according to package directions. Drain pasta and place on individual serving plates. Spoon an equal portion of tomato mixture into the center of each serving of pasta, and garnish with a sprinkle of Parmesan or Asiago cheese, if desired.

Yield: 4 servings

Nature's Way

One antidote to the pressures of college life is simply stepping out into the great outdoors. Like Thoreau's Walden Pond, MSU's arboretum brims with refuges for contemplative solitude. Feeding the ducks is wonderful therapy. So is lollygagging down winding paths, past ponds and fountains. Cross-country skiers have limitless acreage, especially through the farms in south campus. For inspiration, one can scan the historic plaques and designs, like Lee Lawrie's "The Sower," an Art Deco relief on Beaumont Tower that sums up MSU's aspirations: "Whatsoever a man soweth." Some observe stars in Abrams Planetarium and insects up close at the Butterfly House and the Bug House. Also popular are canoe rides, snowman building, even mud volleyball during a downpour. And don't forget the animal births at the College of Veterinary Medicine. Nothing uplifts the spirits quite like their popular traveling show, "The Miracle of Life."

Glacier Spinach Salad

*T*his layered salad recipe from Laura Wilkinson appeared in the MSU Faculty Folk Club's Spartan Specialties *cookbook. Laura, a member of a gourmet group within the Faculty Folk Club, says she got the recipe from her sister, Marylu Spencer.*

12 ounces fresh spinach or romaine lettuce, torn
    into bite-size pieces
12 slices bacon, fried crisp, drained, and crumbled
6 hard-cooked eggs, chopped
1 can (2½ ounces) black olives, drained well
    and sliced
1 sweet onion or 6 to 8 green onions, sliced
1½ cups mayonnaise

1 cup dairy sour cream
½ teaspoon lemon juice
½ teaspoon pepper
¼ teaspoon seasoned salt
½ cup shredded cheddar cheese
Garnishes: Paprika and minced fresh parsley
    (optional)

On a large platter, layer ingredients in this order: spinach or romaine lettuce, bacon, eggs, olives, and onion. In a mixing bowl, combine mayonnaise, sour cream, lemon juice, pepper, and seasoned salt; mix well. Spread mayonnaise mixture evenly over salad ingredients. Cover tightly with plastic wrap and refrigerate for 24 hours. When ready to serve, sprinkle cheese over the salad and garnish with paprika and parsley, if desired. Do not toss. Cut salad into wedges or squares, and serve using a spatula.

Yield: 8 to 10 servings

©CAROLYN SCOTT RISK '01

Tour of the Town

East Lansing is a cozy, vibrant town with its own art and film festivals, parks, outdoor plays and concerts, a fine library, a new aquatic center, a community center, excellent schools, and lots of quaint shops, galleries, bookstores, eateries, and watering holes. It's an integral part of the Michigan State University experience.

Among East Lansing's fifty-one thousand residents are many MSU students, residing in dorms or apartment complexes such as Cedar Village. Downtown merchants cater to a predominantly MSU clientele. The city provides havens for every soul—with a synagogue, mosque, and churches such as St. John's Student Parish and People's Church. Elegant fraternity and sorority houses dot MAC Avenue and the triangle area formed by Grand River and Michigan avenues and Harrison Road.

Rare is the alum for whom nearby neighborhoods, such as Lansing and Okemos, do not provide memories. Many remember hanging out at watering holes such as Crunchy's,

Dagwood's, Harper's (formerly Dooley's), Mac's Bar, The Riviera, or P. T. O'Malleys—or cheering the Spartans on TV at sports bars such as Trippers and Reno's East. Everyone will remember El Azteco, with its huevos rancheros and other authentic Mexican dishes. El Az has moved from a claustrophobic basement to new digs on Albert, where it now has rooftop dining. Also popular are Charlie Kang's, and pizzerias such as Papiano's.

Once in a while, MSU students create a national stir—whether in protest (in 1972, blockading Grand River in response to U.S. actions during the Vietnam War) or in riotous celebration (in 1999, after MSU lost to Duke at the NCAA Final Four in St. Petersburg, Florida). Most of the time, a typical town-and-gown symbiosis prevails, as students enjoy aquatic sports at nearby Lake Lansing and concerts and picnics at spacious Patriache Park.

Now gone from downtown East Lansing are such old favorites as Kewpies, the State Theater, and even Jacobson's. On the other hand, the Curious Book Store lingers on, impervious to the onslaught of retail giants such as Barnes and Noble. Nearing completion are upscale condos on MAC Avenue and Grand River, a first in the downtown landscape.

With the state capital and automotive plants and related industries forming a dynamic urban center next door in Lansing, the home of Michigan State—East Lansing—remains an oasis with its trees, homes, parks, sculptures, banners, shops, and, yes, regular influx of youthful students.

Coral Gables

_____

*C*oral Gables became *the* place for MSU students when it opened in the 1920s. Located just outside the city limits, it could serve beer! During the big band era, names such as Jimmy Dorsey and Glenn Miller played there. In the '60s, students packed its Showbar, dancing to live music by Chubby Checker, Little Richard, and other famous rock bands. Big, beefy MSU football players often worked as bouncers. For quiet conversation, one went downstairs to the Rathskeller, a beer tavern reeking with old-world atmosphere. Many student groups, such as Excalibur, regularly met here. But after East Lansing became wet in 1972, students began to favor watering holes closer to campus. So Alex Vanis, owner since 1968, revamped it as a family restaurant, serving roast turkey and the like. Today, says Alex, many alums revisiting MSU stop by the Gables with their families to savor a bit of nostalgia.

Cinnamon Rolls

*I*t's not only the memories that bring people back to the Coral Gables—it's also the flaky, fresh-baked cinnamon rolls, a best-seller for breakfast.

Rolls	Frosting
1 box (16 ounces) hot roll mix (with yeast)	*⅓ cup water*
1 cup warm water (105–115°F)	*1 tablespoon Karo syrup, warmed*
1 cup sugar	*1 drop vanilla*
1 tablespoon butter, softened	*2 cups confectioners' sugar*
1 tablespoon cinnamon (or to taste)	

To prepare Rolls: In a large mixing bowl, combine hot roll mix (including yeast) and water; using dough hooks, mix on low speed of electric mixer for 10 minutes or until the dough starts to cling together and form a soft ball. Turn dough out onto a lightly floured surface and roll to form a 16x8-inch rectangle, ½-inch thick. In a small bowl, combine sugar, butter, and cinnamon; mix until well blended. Spread creamed mixture evenly over dough. Roll up from one of the long sides, forming a tight, even roll. Using a sharp knife, cut roll into one-inch slices. Place slices on a greased 15x10-inch baking sheet and cover with a clean cloth; set aside to rise for 1 hour.

Preheat oven to 375°F. Bake rolls at 375°F for 20 minutes. Remove pan from oven and cool.

To prepare Frosting: In a mixing bowl, combine water, Karo syrup, and vanilla. Gradually add confectioners' sugar and beat until mixture is smooth and has the desired spreading consistency. Spread frosting over cooled rolls.

Yield: 16 rolls

The Peanut Barrel

With peanut shells littering the floor, a dartboard hanging on the wall, and eccentric signs and paraphernalia sitting on every surface, the Peanut Barrel has the feel of a rustic English village pub. The cozy sidewalk seating area, filled during warm weather with tables and expansive umbrellas, suggests a European outdoor café. This mix of peanut bar and alfresco dining, located in the heart of bustling Grand River Avenue across from Berkey Hall, has attracted hordes of students, professors, intellectuals, alumni, and assorted patrons since it opened in 1973. Famous MSU gadfly Charles "Lash" Larrowe, erstwhile economics professor and *State News* columnist, is a regular who loves to debate the hot political issues of the day over a glass of wine. Some writers and reporters for the *State News,* the student-run daily newspaper, often stroll here for a brew after meeting their deadlines—making this an "extra" special place.

Olive Burger

The Peanut Barrel is known for its big, juicy hamburgers. Owner Joe Bell's favorite is the Olive Burger, a mainstay for a quarter-century.

1 jar (12 ounces) green olives stuffed with pimientos, drained well and sliced

1 cup heavy mayonnaise

2 teaspoons sugar

½ teaspoon lemon juice

1⅓ pounds lean ground beef

4 hamburger buns

Garnish: Dill pickles

In a medium mixing bowl, combine olives, mayonnaise, sugar, and lemon juice; mix well. Cover and refrigerate until thoroughly chilled.

Form ground beef into four ⅓-pound burgers. Cook burgers to desired doneness on a griddle or in a skillet. Place each burger on the bottom half of a bun, then top with a large scoop of olive mixture. Serve sandwich open-faced, with the top of the bun on the side. Garnish with a dill pickle.

Yield: 4 servings

Beggar's Banquet

Bob Adler (with his signature beard) has hosted Beggar's Banquet since 1973, when he opened the restaurant across from campus "to provide good food and a welcome ambience for everyone." Since then, Bob has nurtured an eclectic milieu where MSU students gather under the Tiffany lamps along with artists, governors, supreme court justices, lobbyists, department chairs, and professors for one common purpose: "Gimme eat." The most popular item? "Sympathy for the Devil" Beef Chili—a favorite since it first appeared on the menu, and guaranteed to generate fireworks like every day is the Fourth of July. Lots of art pieces and photographs by local artists add to the atmospherics, as does the occasional arrival of some customers via limousine, perhaps to discuss serious state business. Says Yvonne Nystrom Bean, a student employee in the '80s, "Every time I hear Billy Joel's 'Piano Man,' I think of Beggar's Banquet."

Beef Chili

*B*eggar's Banquet offers a numerical Chili Rating based on the Richter scale—and then very thought-fully serves up a seventy-five-cent "Sympathy for the Customer" beer with the chili.

---

8 pounds beef stew meat

12 cups coarsely chopped onions

6 cups chopped jalapeños

5 cans (No. 10; 12½ cups each) tomatoes

1 quart cider vinegar

¾ cup finely chopped garlic

½ cup dried oregano leaves

½ cup ground cumin seed

5 cans (No. 10; 12½ cups each) kidney beans

Combine all ingredients except kidney beans in a ten-gallon pot; mix well. Bring to a boil, then reduce heat to low. Cover pot and simmer, stirring frequently, for 3 to 4 hours or until the meat is very tender. Add beans and simmer for another hour.

Yield: about 50 servings

Note: To serve a smaller crowd (14 to 16), the above quantities can be reduced to the following amounts:

2 pounds beef stew meat

3 cups coarsely chopped onions

1½ cups chopped jalapeños

2 cans (14 ounces each) tomatoes

½ cup cider vinegar

3 tablespoons finely chopped garlic

2 tablespoons dried oregano leaves

2 tablespoons ground cumin seed

2 cans (14 ounces each) kidney beans

©Carolyn Scott Risk '01

Dusty's Cellar

A paradise for gourmets, Dusty's Cellar combines the atmosphere of a European bistro with contemporary American cuisine. Daily, the aromas of fresh French bread, tortes, pastries, and muffins waft from its bakery, which opened in 1980 along with a retail store for gourmet foods, fine wine, and beer. Founder Dusty Rhodes, an oenophile who sharpened his culinary tastes while working in London, Paris, Rome, Hong Kong, and Tokyo as the longtime president of UPI television news, says the restaurant grew from a demonstration kitchen in his store that had become popular beyond belief. True epicures from MSU don't mind the drive to nearby Okemos for an exceptional meal at Dusty's, where they can also buy fine wines and lots of goodies, such as imported chocolates. Dusty, who served for many years as the PA announcer in Spartan Stadium, has clearly scored a touchdown!

Smoked Turkey Torta Rustica

*D*usty Rhodes says, *"From day one, Torta Rustica has been the best-seller at Dusty's Cellar. We got the idea from the countryside in Tuscany, where men would take it to the fields wrapped in newspapers, like miners and their pasties [in Cornwall]."*

---

4 pounds brioche dough (or frozen bread dough, thawed), divided

2 pounds provolone cheese, sliced and divided into four equal portions

1½ pounds peppered turkey breast, cubed

2 cans (14 ounces each) artichoke hearts, drained and strained through a sieve

2 pounds ricotta cheese

4 tablespoons chopped fresh garlic

1 tablespoon dried basil leaves

1 tablespoon dried oregano leaves

1 teaspoon freshly grated nutmeg

1 teaspoon salt

1 pound spinach leaves, sautéed in 2 tablespoons olive oil, then strained through a sieve (drain well)

4 tablespoons (2 ounces) pine nuts, toasted (See Note)

1 pound sweet red peppers, grilled, halved, and seeded (See Note)

Egg wash (1 egg beaten with 1 to 2 tablespoons water), as needed

---

Prepare all ingredients before starting to assemble torta. Spray a twelve-inch springform pan with nonstick cooking spray. Preheat oven to 375°F.

On a floured surface, roll 3 pounds of dough into a circle fourteen inches in diameter and ¼- to ½-inch thick. Line springform pan with dough, letting one inch of the dough hang over the sides of the pan. Layer one-fourth of the provolone over the dough. Spread turkey and artichokes over the cheese.

In a mixing bowl, combine ricotta, garlic, basil, oregano, nutmeg, and salt; mix well. Spoon ricotta mixture evenly over turkey and artichokes. Layer one-fourth of the provolone over ricotta mixture. Press provolone firmly to remove air pockets. Spread spinach evenly over provolone. Sprinkle pine nuts over spinach. Layer one-fourth of the provolone over spinach and pine nuts. Arrange peppers over provolone, then cover peppers with remaining provolone.

 Roll remaining dough into a circle twelve inches in diameter and ¼- to ½-inch thick. Place dough over torta, and seal edges by rolling up overhanging bottom dough and pinching it together with the top dough. Trim away any excess dough. Brush top of torta with egg wash. Bake at 375°F for 15 minutes, then cover torta with foil and bake 45 to 50 minutes longer. Remove from oven and cool completely.

 When ready to serve, preheat oven to 350°F. Use a sharp knife to cut cooled torta into twelve wedges. Place wedges on a baking sheet and reheat at 350°F for 20 to 30 minutes. Serve with a crisp garden salad or a fresh fruit salad.

Yield: 12 servings

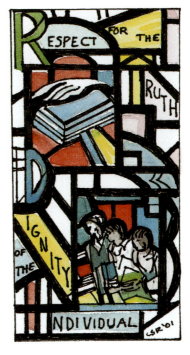

Note: To toast fresh pine nuts, spread nuts on a baking sheet and bake at 300°F for about 8 to 10 minutes or until nuts are golden brown. Watch closely as nuts can burn quickly.

To prepare red peppers, roast over an open flame or place under broiler until skin blisters and turns black. Set aside to cool. Peel burned skin from peppers, then halve peppers and remove seeds.

Epilogue

An MSU degree is treasured by more than 350,000 Spartans around the globe, including Michigan's last two governors, John Engler (elected in 1990) and James Blanchard (1982–90), and U.S. senators Debbie Stabenow (elected in 2000) and Spence Abraham (1994–2000).

Graduates receive their diplomas along with inspiration from speakers such as Elie Wiesel, Stephen Jay Gould, or Doris Kearns Goodwin. The class of 1995 heard President Bill Clinton urge them to "redeem the promise that is America." Most students pay attention, even though sprinkled on caps are pithy messages such as "Thanks, Mom & Dad" and "I Can Now Rite!"

Emotions and tears invariably pour out like champagne from bottles, a cumulative result of so much underlying effort and sacrifice. In 2001, seniors Charlie Bell, Mike Chappell, Andre Hutson, Brandon Smith, and David Thomas—members of the winningest class in Big Ten basketball history with 115 wins—capped their three straight Final Fours and four straight Big Ten championships with MSU sheepskins.

New grads join the ranks of alumni (as mailings from the alumni office remind them). It's an enviable status. A 2001 survey by the *Wall Street Journal* ranks MSU grads among the nation's most desirable by corporate recruiters. No wonder. Top achievers in virtually every field include Spartans. In the auto industry, Spartans have been CEOs of Daimler-Chrysler (James Holden), Ford Motor Company (Alexander Trotman), General Motors (Robert Stemple), Mazda (Bill Miller), and Toyota of North America (Gary Convis). They include major successes such as Thomas Bailey, founder of the Janus Fund; Drayton McLane, owner of the Houston Astros; and Robin Richards, chairman and CEO of MP3.com.

In film, new grads will find a World Wide Web of Spartans—as studio CEOs (Bill Mechanic at Twentieth Century Fox, Frank Price at Universal and Columbia), directors (Walter Hill, Sam Raimi), writers (Jim Cash, Jack Epps, Jr.), actors (James Caan, Anthony Heald, Robert Urich), or producers (Ed Feldman, Mike Lobell, Warren Zide). Basketball legend Magic Johnson, who has built movie complexes in many cities, even boasts his own star on Hollywood's Walk of Fame.

No matter what the field, every new MSU grad should try to reach for the stars. To them, we say, "Go Green!"

©Carolyn Scott Risk '01

MSU School Songs

MSU Alma Mater
("MSU Shadows")

MSU we love thy shadows When twilight silence falls,
Flushing deep and softly paling O'er ivy covered halls;
Beneath the pines we'll gather To give our faith so true,
Sing our love for Alma Mater And thy praises MSU.

When from these scenes we wander
　　And twilight shadows fade,
Our memory still will linger
　　Where light and shadows played;
In the evening oft we'll gather And pledge our faith anew,
Sing our love for Alma Mater And thy praises MSU.

The song was written in 1927 by Bernard P. Traynor, football line coach. The tune is derived from the opera Lucia di Lammermoor *by Donizetti. In 1949, this became MSU's alma mater when students voted overwhelmingly in its favor. Because MSU was MSC at the time, the original lines read: "Beneath the pines we'll gather To give our hearts to thee, Sing our love for Alma Mater And thy praises MSC."*

MSU Fight Song

On the banks of the Red Cedar Is a school that's known to all,
Its specialty is winning, And those Spartans play good ball,
Spartan teams are never beaten, All thru the game they fight,
Fight for the only colors, Green and White,

Go right thru for MSU, Watch the points keep growing,
Spartan teams are bound to win, They're fighting with a vim,
　　Rah! Rah! Rah!
See their team is weakening, We're going to win the game,
Fight! Fight! Rah! Team Fight! Victory for MSU,
Up with the colors, Unfurl them on high!
　　Fight! Rah! Team Fight!

The song was penned in 1915 by Francis Irving Lankey, a Spartan "yellmaster," who was inspired by MSU's back-to-back upsets against Michigan and Wisconsin in 1913. He wanted MSU to have a song comparable to "On Wisconsin" and Michigan's "The Victors." A member of the class of 1916, Lankey joined the military and died in 1918 during a World War I mission. A memorial plaque honoring Lankey lies outside Spartan Stadium's north tunnel.

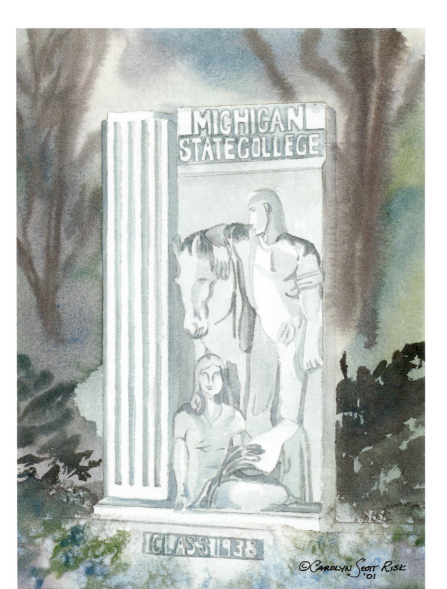

MSU Historical Timeline

Note: "MSU" is used to denote the school throughout this timeline.

1855   Agricultural College of the State of Michigan is founded.

1861   The school's name is changed to State Agricultural College.

1862   President Abraham Lincoln signs the Morrill Act, which allows states to fund colleges through sales of land. MSU emerges as the prototype land-grant college.

1870   First coeds (ten of them) are admitted; twenty-six years later, a women's program (which would evolve into the College of Human Ecology) is established.

1876   The Farmer's Institute, forerunner of agricultural extension, is established.

1884   First intercollegiate athletic competition (baseball, vs. Olivet).

1888   Agricultural Experiment Station is established.

1907   Commencement speaker Theodore Roosevelt is the first U.S. president to speak at MSU. (President Bill Clinton would speak at MSU in 1995.)

1909   The school's name is changed to Michigan Agricultural College. / Agriculture Hall is built.

1912   First county agricultural agents are named; two years later, the Smith-Lever Act would provide federal funds for Cooperative Extension Service.

1916   Automaker R. E. Olds gives $100,000 to MSU—the first private donation for a campus building (Olds Hall).

1922   WKAR-AM radio goes on the air. (FM radio would follow in 1948, and TV in 1954.)

1925   The school's name is changed to Michigan State College of Agriculture and Applied Science. / The first doctoral degree is conferred. / The MSU Union is dedicated in memory of American soldiers who died while serving their country.

1926   The school's nickname, Spartans, is coined by a sportswriter.

1929   Beaumont Tower, a symbol for the university, is dedicated.

1935   The Alumni Association turns over the MSU Union to the university.

1941   John A. Hannah, who would spearhead MSU's stunning growth from agricultural college to global research megaversity, becomes the school's twelfth president.

1944   University College is established (it would be disbanded in 1980).

1945   Sparty ceramic statue is unveiled. / Postwar building boom is launched, reaching $50 million in the next decade.

1949   MSU is admitted to the Big Ten athletic conference. / "MSU Shadows" becomes the official alma mater after a student vote.

1951   The Kellogg Center for Continuing Education is founded; a hotel and conference center would open the next year.

1952   College of Education is established. / Alumni Memorial Chapel is built. / MSU wins its first national football title; two years later, it would win its first Rose Bowl.

1955   In the school's centennial year, its name is changed to Michigan State University of Agriculture and Applied Science. / College of Communication Arts and Sciences, the first of its kind in nation, is established. / U.S. postage stamp commemorates MSU as a pioneer land-grant college.

1957   Honors College is created for high-achieving students.

1959   Oakland University opens under MSU's aegis at Meadow Brook Farms. (In 1971, OU would gain independence.)

1962   Colleges of Arts and Letters, Natural Science, and Social Science are established from the College of Science and Arts.

1963   MSU enrolls more freshman Merit Scholars than any other institution in the nation.

1964   The school's name is changed to Michigan State University. / MSU is admitted to the prestigious Association of American Universities. / Abrams Planetarium opens.

1965   The first campus residential college, where students live and have classes mostly in the same residence hall, is established.

1966   The College of Human Medicine opens, followed by the College of Osteopathic Medicine in 1971. / MSU wins its first NCAA hockey championship (second championship would come in 1986).

1975   Management Education Center opens in Troy.

1979   Led by Magic Johnson, MSU wins its first NCAA basketball title, beating Larry Bird and Indiana State University in Salt Lake City (second title would come in 2000, when MSU beats Florida in Indianapolis).

1982   National Superconducting Cyclotron Laboratory and Wharton Center for Performing Arts are dedicated.

1986   Plant Soil and Sciences Building is dedicated.

1987   Michigan Festival and MSU Museum's Festival of Michigan Folklife (now Great Lakes Folk Festival) make their debuts.

1989   Jack Breslin Student Events Center is dedicated. / MSU Libraries launches MAGIC, its automated system. / An Alumni Lifelong Education division, first in the Big Ten, is created within the MSU Alumni Association.

1991   Alumnus Eli Broad pledges $20 million—the largest gift ever to a public university.

1992   The academic calendar shifts to semesters, and registration becomes fully computerized. / MSU hosts the final U.S. presidential debate with George Bush, Bill Clinton, and Ross Perot.

1993 MSU's first capital campaign raises $217.8 million, surpassing the goal. / Horticultural Demonstration Gardens and the North Business Complex are dedicated.

1994 MSU Safe Place, the first domestic-abuse shelter on a college campus, opens. / Tuition Guarantee limits tuition increases to the rate of inflation.

1996 The Detroit College of Law affiliates with MSU. / Beaumont Tower carillons are restored. / The Pavilion for Agriculture and Livestock Education opens.

1997 Merillat Equine Center in Adrian is given to MSU. / Major addition to Engineering Building is dedicated. / NBA basketball player Steve Smith's $2.5 million gift is the largest ever by a pro athlete to an alma mater. / MSU Study Abroad becomes the nation's largest foreign study program, with 1,454 students in 105 programs throughout 45 countries.

1999 MSU becomes a key player in Michigan's billion-dollar Life Science Corridor—a statewide project to invest in and promote life sciences research and business development.

2001 Nearing completion: Biomedical and Physical Sciences Center, SOAR 4.2-meter telescope in Chilean Andes, and Executive Development Center.

Annual Events at MSU

January   Kresge Art Museum's Masterworks Exhibition / Martin Luther King Day Celebration and Festivities

February   MSU Museum's Chocolate Party / Native American Indian Student Organization's Pow-Wow of Love / State of the University Address / Susan B. Anthony Celebration

March   Agriculture and Natural Resources (ANR) Week / East Lansing Film Festival / Jazz Spectacular / Master of Fine Arts Show at Kresge Art Museum / School of Music's Spring Opera / Taste of the Town / Vet-A-Visit at College of Veterinary Science

April   Kaleidoscope: A Day For Women / Les Gourmets, by students of The School of Hospitality Business / MSU Libraries' Student Book Collection Competition / Senior Student Receptions at Cowles House / Small Animals Day at the Pavilion / Undergraduate Show at Kresge Art Museum

May   East Lansing Arts Festival / MSU Union Arts and Crafts Show / Spring Commencements

June–July   Ag Expo / 4-H Exploration Days / Muelder International Summer Carillon Recital Series / Patriarchs' Reunion / Summer Circle Theatre (on the banks of the Red Cedar) / Summer Sports Camps

August   Academic Orientation for Freshmen / Cars on Campus (Charity Concours d'Elegance, Grand River Cruise For Kids, and MSU Safe Place Reception, Dinner, and Auction) / Football Family Fun Day / MSU Museum's Great Lakes Folk Festival

September   Spartan Spirit in Spartan Stadium / Kresge Art Museum's Twilight in the Garden

October   Student Alumni Foundation's Family Weekend / Homecoming (Green and White Luncheon, Parade, Class Reunions) / MSU Museum Dinosaur Dash / Spartan Spectacular Marching Band Concert

November   Autumnfest at the Pavilion / Global Festival at MSU Union / Midnight Mania at Breslin Center

December   Fall Commencements / Spartan Coca-Cola Classic Basketball Tournament

For more events on the MSU calendar, call 517.355.1855, or visit http://events.msu.edu.
For MSU alumni events, call 517.355.8314, or visit http://www.msualum.com.

Index